SPEAK, READ & WRITE

technical english

NOW

Casting & Wheel Manufacturing

Leyva – Acosta – Thomas – Gutiérrez

www.speaktechnicalnow.com

Idea Editorial – www.ideaeditorial.com
Translapró – www.translapro.com
José Luis Leyva, Marissa Gutiérrez, Daniela Acosta, Roberto Gutiérrez, Alberto Rojas
Illustrations by Melissa Gutiérrez

ISBN: 1542310229
ISBN 13: 978-1542310222

PREFACE

Speak, Read and Write Technical English is the perfect textbook for Industrial and Business applications. This series of textbooks will enable *English as a Second Language* students to apply language learning to their work environment. The language learning platform (including the online lessons) allows the employees of various industries to perform in English language at their jobs. Areas of specialization include aerospace, automotive, electrical/electronics, medical, casting and wheel manufacturing, CNC precision tools, legal and other. Look for our ESL industry specialized English courses at your location and other textbooks from the same series at www.speaktechnicalnow.com

Table of Contents

Unit 1 | Lesson 1
A Visit from Corporate

Listen to this lesson's audio in the course's webpage.

John:	Good Morning, Mr. Scott. Welcome to our plant. My name is John and my coworker's name is Sandy.
Mr. Scott:	
Sandy:	Good morning, John and Sandy. Thank you very much.
John:	We are part of the Human Resources Team. Later, we will show you the areas of the
Mr. Scott:	plant, as well as the safety rules that we have.
	We will also provide the personal protective equipment that you need to wear when you are at the plant.
	Great! Nice meeting you

Tell your co-workers about yourself. Introduce yourself to other people. Say your name, title, department and activities related to your job position. Say who your boss is and if you supervise other employees.

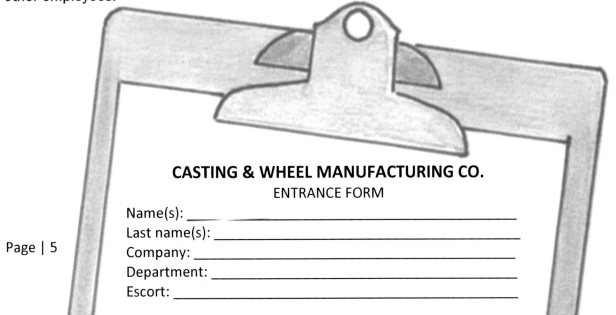

CASTING & WHEEL MANUFACTURING CO.
ENTRANCE FORM

Name(s): _____

Last name(s): _____

Company: _____

Department: _____

Escort: _____

1. Work in pairs. You are visiting a plant outside of the country. Work with your partner to answer the following questions. Write down the answers. Ask each other to spell names and last names. At the end of the activity you will introduce your partner to the class.

What's your name?

_____

Where are you from?

_____

What is your department?

_____

What is your job position?

_____

Who is your supervisor?

_____

What are your functions in the company?

_____

Do you interact with any other departments?

_____

How long have you worked for the company?

_____

Spell the following names:

JONES, ANDREA
MIYAMOTO, SATORU
RODRIGUEZ, ESTEBAN
FORMIER, EMANUELLE
TIANG, YU
FEIGENBAUM, HANS

2. After the session, write a short paragraph indicating your name and last name, title (job position) and activities you perform at the plant/office.

Start with something like:

Hello, my name is _____ and I work at the _____ department. I'm _____ (title/job position). My supervisor's name is _____

NOTES:

VOCABULARY:

Unit 1 | Lesson 2
The Workplace

Listen to this lesson's audio in the course's webpage.

Read the general rules for the plant and match them with the signs below by using numbers.

Rules:
1. Use the designated pedestrian walkways or areas.
2. No cell phones.
3. No running or horseplay.
4. Use the appropriate protective clothing.
5. Don't drink or eat in the production area.
6. Always follow the safety signs.

Answer the following questions. Then, see the chart below. Discuss what each shape and color mean and complete it.

Why do you think it's important to follow the safety signs?

What rules can you think of that are very emphasized in your department?

What is the strangest safety rule you have heard?

Geometric Shape	Meaning	Color	Examples in the Workplace
🚫			
△			
●			
■			
▬			

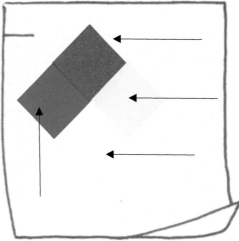

Work in pairs, write six more rules that you use in your department or work position. Try to think of uncommon or strange rules. Everyone will share their rules with the group.

NOTES:

VOCABULARY:

Unit 1 | Lesson 3
Protective Equipment

Listen to this lesson's audio in the course's webpage.

Read the following dialogue.

Mr. Scott:	I would like you to show me the type of PPE that you use here.
John:	Of course Mr. Scott.
Sandy:	We keep the equipment here in the company in the best conditions.
John:	First of all, as you can see all of our employees are wearing Level D protection. That is, their work uniform including coveralls, aprons and coats.
Sandy:	Everyone is required to wear safety shoes, including steel toed shoes. Depending on their work, they have to wear gloves, a hard hat, safety glasses.
John:	We also have equipment ready for working on heights, like harnesses.
Sandy:	Finally, we have Level A, B and C equipment like self-contained breathing apparatus approved by OSHA and NIOSH.
Mr. Scott:	Excellent, Thank you.

Work in pairs and then work as one group.
Describe the following personal protective equipment items using it is, they are, etc.

Match the picture with the correct name and discuss in what situations would you need to use this PPE.

- Steel toe shoes

- Safety glasses

- Earplugs

- Hard cap

- Safety gloves

- Self-Contained Breath Apparatus

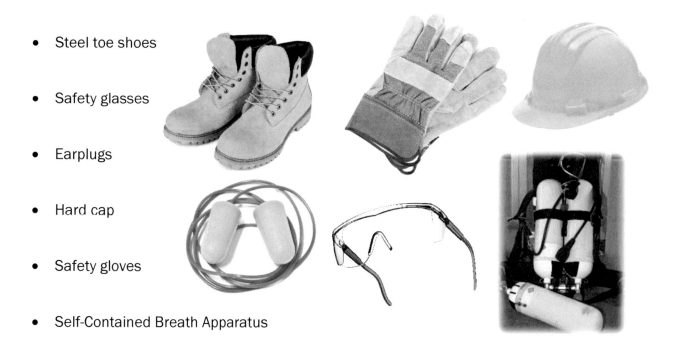

 WRITE

Write other personal protective equipment items that you have at the plant/office/facility.

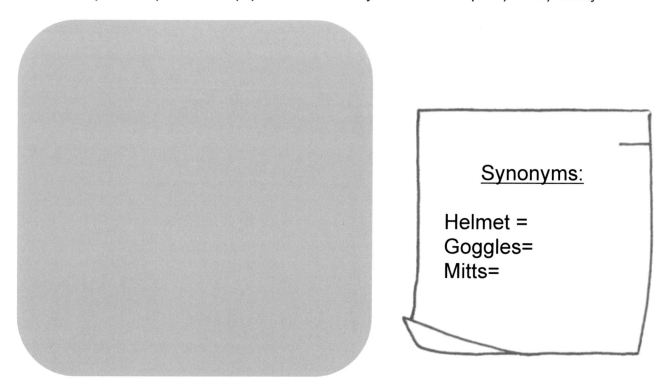

Synonyms:

Helmet =
Goggles=
Mitts=

NOTES:

VOCABULARY:

Unit 1 | Lesson 4 Schedules

Listen to this lesson's audio in the course's webpage.

Read the schedule below and fill the blanks with the hours and activities that the instructor will tell you.

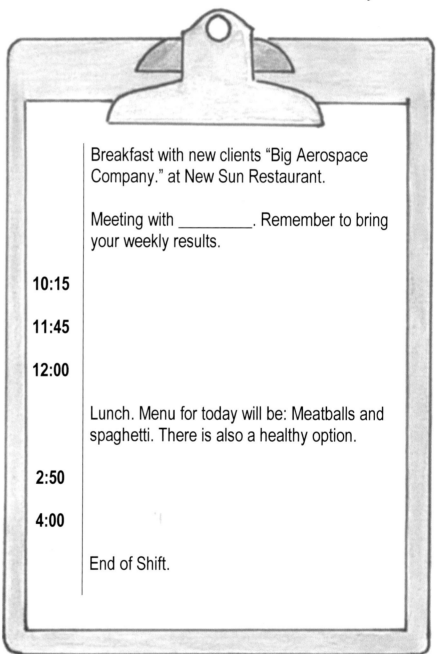

Breakfast with new clients "Big Aerospace Company." at New Sun Restaurant.

Meeting with _____. Remember to bring your weekly results.

10:15

11:45

12:00

Lunch. Menu for today will be: Meatballs and spaghetti. There is also a healthy option.

2:50

4:00

End of Shift.

What is your usual schedule?

At what time do the shifts change?

At what time do you go to eat?

Do you have any activities after work?

What do you do on Sundays and Saturdays?

Do you have a set time for meetings?

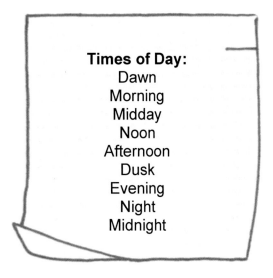

Times of Day:
Dawn
Morning
Midday
Noon
Afternoon
Dusk
Evening
Night
Midnight

Write down the activities you normally do during a day, inside and outside of work. Include hours and/or times of day.

NOTES:

VOCABULARY:

Unit 2 | Lesson 1
Showing the Plant

Listen to this lesson's audio in the course's webpage.

Observe the map and identify each room according to what you listen in the dialogue.

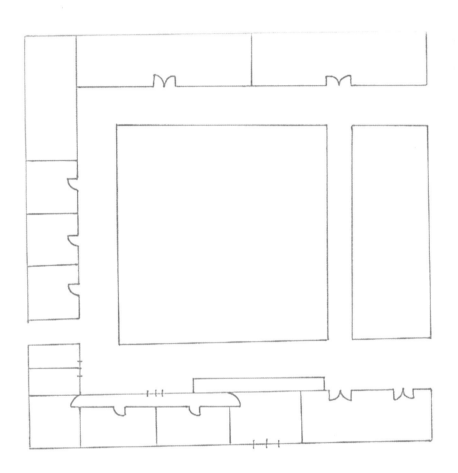

Read the sentences and complete them. Discuss them and see if the answers vary.

The _____ is where we can have our meetings and conferences.

The_____ is where we all eat.

The _____ is where our product is manufactured.

The _____ is where our products are checked for quality.

The _____ is where we wait for an escort to enter the plant.

The _____ is where we assemble the parts.

The _____ is where we store materials.

Think about the following questions:

What other rooms can you find in your plant?
What are the rooms you go to the most and why?
What differences can you find between this plant and yours?
What areas are outside the plant?
Does your production area have any subsections? Which ones?
What other administrative offices are in your plant?

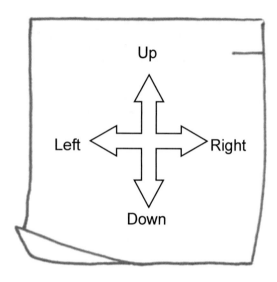

Imagine you have to show a visitor where he/she can find you. Start from the lobby and give instructions (for example: go right, left, continue straight, upstairs, downstairs, across, at the end, at the back, at the center, etc.)

NOTES:

VOCABULARY:

Unit 2 | Lesson 2
At the Warehouse

Listen to this lesson's audio in the course's webpage.

Observe the image below and answer the questions from the instructor.

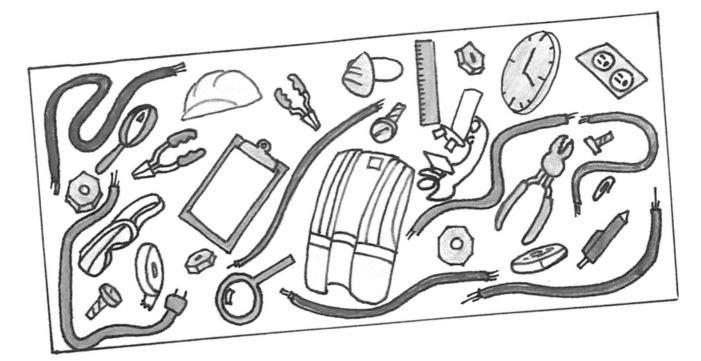

Complete with is/are.

1. There __ many red cables, but we don't have many blue ones.
2. There __ a lot of noise in the plant, I think a machine is not working.
3. There __ not much oxygen in the tank, we will need a refill.
4. There ___ many wheels we need to return. Those are not safe!
5. There ___ not many employees today because it is a national holiday.
6. ___ there water in this container?
7. ___ there any gloves in that box?

Look at this table with countable vs uncountable nouns. Fill it out with the examples on the right and suggest more examples. Discuss.

Countable / Uncountable

Examples:

Nitrogen, units, sets, compressed air, energy, tools, water, machines, material.

WRITE

Write 4 sentences using the countable and uncountable nouns above and there is and there are.

NOTES:

VOCABULARY:

Unit 2 | Lesson 3
A Meeting

Listen to this lesson's audio in the course's webpage.

Read the dialogue bubbles and number the comic boxes in the correct order.

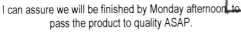

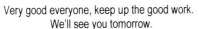

1. Work in pairs. You're in a meeting with your supervisor. Tell him or her about the project you're currently working on. As you listen to your partner give them your opinion about the work they are doing.

2. As a group, listen to each participant share their current projects. Ask them questions using what, where, when, why, who or how.

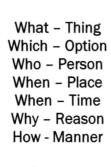

What – Thing
Which – Option
Who – Person
When – Place
When – Time
Why – Reason
How - Manner

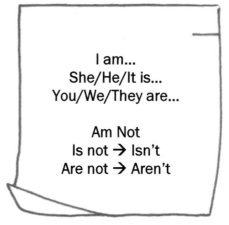

I am...
She/He/It is...
You/We/They are...

Am Not
Is not → Isn't
Are not → Aren't

As a group, come up with a problem that the plant is facing. Write a short paragraph in which you propose a solution.

NOTES:

VOCABULARY:

Unit 2 | Lesson 4
Checking Production Reports

Listen to your partner's presentations and take notes below.

Read the following production report.

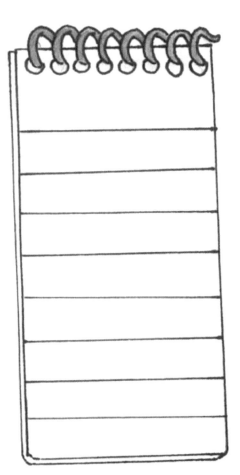

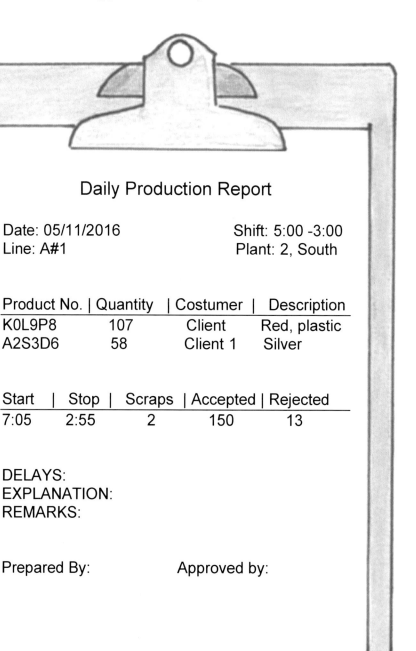

Daily Production Report

Date: 05/11/2016   Shift: 5:00 -3:00
Line: A#1   Plant: 2, South

Product No.	Quantity	Costumer	Description
K0L9P8	107	Client	Red, plastic
A2S3D6	58	Client 1	Silver

Start	Stop	Scraps	Accepted	Rejected
7:05	2:55	2	150	13

DELAYS:
EXPLANATION:
REMARKS:

Prepared By: Approved by:

 SPEAK

As a group, discuss what reports you have to present to your supervisor or manager.

Do you have weekly or monthly reports?

How do you present your reports?

Do you collaborate with anyone to carry out the reports?

Have you ever had a situation when you couldn't finish a report?

Have you ever had a situation when you missed something on your report?

 WRITE

Write about a situation in which you had to present an emergency report? What was the situation? To whom did you have to present it? What was the report about?

Regular Verbs:

-ed ending

Examples:
Check → Checked
Call → Called
Finish → Finished

Irregular Verbs:

Endings vary.

Examples:
Is → Was
Find → Found
Break → Broken

NOTES:

VOCABULARY:

Unit 3 | Lesson 1
A Search for New Employees

Listen to this lesson's audio in the course's webpage.

Read the following description of a candidate. Is he/she someone your company would like to hire?
Complete the resume below with your own information.

B.S. in Manufacturing Engineering from ABC University. I have the Certification in Wheel Mould Production. I am proficient in AutoCAD, Microsoft Office, SAP MM. I speak fluent English and basic French. I have seven years of experience in the field. I am a creative person. I have experience with prototyping and theoretical research. I have excellent communication and management skills. I also have soldering experience, and I am willing to work alone or in a team. I am also willing to relocate.

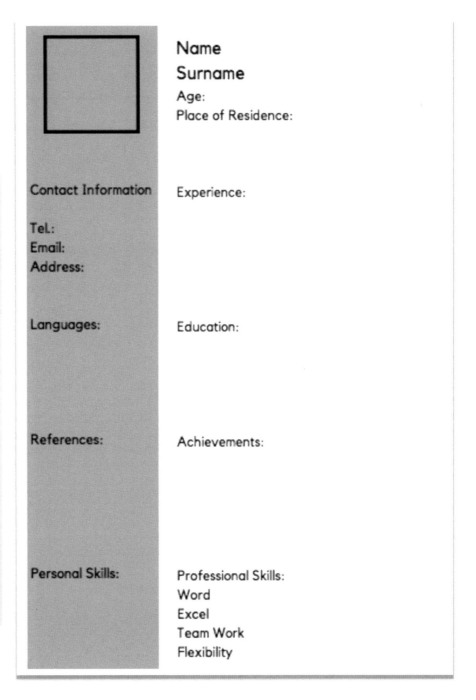

Name
Surname
Age:
Place of Residence:

Contact Information

Tel:
Email:
Address:

Experience:

Languages:

Education:

References:

Achievements:

Personal Skills:

Professional Skills:
Word
Excel
Team Work
Flexibility

Work in pairs. Interview your partner. Ask each other the following questions.

1. Tell me about yourself.
2. What are your strengths?
3. What are your weaknesses?
4. What do you know about this industry?
5. Are you willing to relocate or move?
6. Where do you see yourself in five years?
7. What would be your ideal work environment?
8. What do you like to do?
9. How would you describe yourself in three words?
10. What can you bring to the position that other candidates cannot?

Character Traits:
Organized
Competitive
Patient
Responsible
Friendly
Fair
Ambitious
Active
Adventurous

Write a summary or description of yourself and your work, including past experience, schooling, special certifications, etc.

NOTES:

VOCABULARY:

Unit 3 | Lesson 2
Hiring

Listen to this lesson's audio in the course's webpage.

Read the following dialogue.

John:	Hey Sandy, we have three people coming in tomorrow, can we go over the list of documents they need?
Sandy:	Give me just a second; I need to finish writing this e-mail.
John:	What are you sending?
Sandy:	Just the memo about the upcoming holiday.
John:	Oh, that's right.
Sandy:	Okay, finished. What did you need?
John:	Can we go over the list of documents that we need from the three candidates?
Sandy:	Yes, yes, yes. Let's see. They need their birth certificate, copy of their official identification, a medical exam from the Red Cross, a copy of their Resume, two recommendation letters, a No-Criminal History letter, CURP...
John:	If they have INFONAVIT or IMSS they need to bring in their number so we can register them.
Sandy:	Right. We also need their studies certifications, anything from a copy of their degree or their professional license or professional identification card.
John:	We also need a proof of residence that can be anything from their water bill to their property tax receipt.
Finally, we need their Federal Tax Payer ID.
Sandy:	Great, I think we're ready. Thanks.
John:	

c

As a group discuss the following questions.
Have you ever gotten a rejection call?
What do you do if a job doesn't call you back?
Have you ever been asked for any other important document?
Why do you think these documents are important for HR?
For internal hiring, how do you let the person know they received the job position?
How much time should candidates have to gather the important documents?
What else do you think is important during the hiring process?

Pretend that someone has asked you for a recommendation letter. Write a "mock" or fake letter recommending that person for a job position.

Commonly Used Phrases in Formal Letters:

- To whom it may concern...
- Dear Mr./Ms./Mrs.

- With respect to...
- Regarding...
- I am writing in behalf of...

- I look forward to hearing from you...
- Please feel free to contact me if...

- Kind regards,
- Sincerely,
- Yours faithfully,

Positive Adjectives:
Able
Brilliant
Trustworthy
Hard-working
Efficient
Intelligent
Decisive
Bold
Honest

NOTES:

VOCABULARY:

Unit 3 | Lesson 3
Forms of Payment & Holidays

Listen to your partner's presentation.

Read the following note.

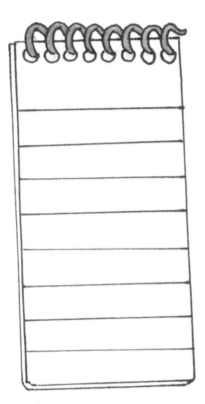

Hi, Sandy.
Could you give me a call?
I have been hearing rumors about our payroll changing from biweekly into monthly. Is this true? When does it start?

I was talking with Tom from Finance and they already authorized the punctuality bonuses!

Also, we have to organize the celebration for the Company's 50th anniversary. I have some ideas I want to share with you. Maybe we can do it the same way that we celebrated mother's day, in the plant's cafeteria with a nice catering service. What do you think?

- John.

Discuss the following questions:

How does your company handle mandatory holidays?
Companies can pay weekly, biweekly or monthly. What is your company's form of payment? Which do you think is the best for employees: weekly payment, biweekly payment or monthly payment?
Have you ever worked on a mandatory holiday?
What other days off does your company handle?
Have you ever worked in a company that had any other rest days?
Have you ever worked in a company that worked 365 days a year? What was the reason?

Observe the calendar below and answer the instructor's questions.

January	February	March	April
	National Holiday		Family Day

May	June	July	August
Mother's Day Celebration	Company's 50th Anniversary		

September	October	November	December
	Work Day		New Year's Celebration

You are working in HR. Write a memo in which you tell the employees that a mandatory holiday has been moved. For example, May 1st falls or is on a Wednesday. The company has decided that the rest day will be moved to the following Friday. Write a memo for the employees explaining why the rest day has been moved.

- Week, Quarter, Semester, Year.
- Biweekly, Bimonthly, Biannually.
- Quarterly, Annually, Yearly.

NOTES:

VOCABULARY:

Unit 3 | Lesson 4 Training

Listen to this lesson's audio in the course's webpage.

Read the checklist. As a group, discuss what you think each training program will deal with. Then, in your own book, check which training programs are pertinent to your job position.

Hello, everyone! Are you ready for your training?

☐ 1. Getting to know the emergency procedures
☐ 2. Knowing your PPE
☐ 3. Reviewing the job requirements and evaluation parameters
☐ 4. Touring the facility entirely
☐ 5. Recognizing your computer systems
☐ 6. Cleaning the equipment and checking the operation
☐ 7. Establishing company rules, regulations and standards
☐ 8. Understanding state and federal regulations
☐ 9. Resolving conflicts and managing a team
☐ 10. Learning how to perform employee or department reviews
☐ 11. Learning how to conduct an interview
☐ 12. Carrying out imports and exports
☐ 13. Meeting foreign visitors
☐ 14. Operating industrial transport efficiently
☐ 15. Inspecting equipment systematically
☐ 16. Inspecting and approving finished products
☐ 17. Interpreting drawings accurately
☐ 18. Working with English documents
☐ 19. Disposing correctly of chemical waste
☐ 20. Reading an MSDS
☐ 21. Programming units and devices successfully

Discuss the following questions.

What do you remember about your training when you first started in your company?

What other important things did you have?

What else do you think is important to know when you begin a new job?

What other type of training is available for you in your company and job position?

How important do you think training is, in your personal experience?

ADVERBS OF MANNER – ENDING IN LY

- Consistently
- Effectively
- Repeatedly
- Slowly
-
-

Do you know your company's vision and mission?
Write them in your own words.
What do these things mean to you professionally?
Do you have any special certifications? Which ones?

NOTES:

VOCABULARY:

Unit 4 | Lesson 1
Incoming Inspection

Listen to this lesson's audio in the course's webpage.

Read the following dialogue.

John:	Here we make sure all our components are OK for production.
Mr. Scott:	Do you check all the shipments from the suppliers?
Sandy:	Yes, we do.
John:	However, we create the sampling plan based on the specifications.
Mr. Scott:	And, how do you determine the sampling plan?
John:	The sampling plan is determined around the quality of the supplier. If the supplier always sends good quality the sample is smaller. If we have a supplier that always sends defects we have a bigger sample.
Mr. Scott:	So, what is the biggest sample that you use?
Sandy:	The biggest sample is 100%.
Mr. Scott:	Excellent. What happens if you have defective material?
Sandy:	We must also check that good material is not contaminated, so we send defective material to quarantine.
John:	If the material is OK, then we send it to the warehouse.
Sandy:	But, some components are sent to the QC lab where they're tested.
Mr. Scott:	Great, what type of components do you receive?
Sandy:	We receive aluminum bars. Aluminum is the main component of our wheels.
Mr. Scott:	What do we need to have to get the components here?
Sandy:	We will see that with the Logistics department.
John:	The next stop is the customs and traffic area.

As a group, discuss what the incoming inspection process is for your company. What are the quality specifications? What gauge of wires do you receive? What tools do you use to carry out your inspections processes? **Work in pairs, ask and answer questions about the incoming inspection process, or go to the incoming inspection and talk to the employees there.**

Comparative Adjectives:
- er ending for short words
More + adjective for long words

Superlative Adjectives:
- est ending for short words
most + adjective for long words

ex: smaller than → the smallest
more efficient than→ the most efficient

Write a short paragraph in which you describe the incoming inspection process of your company. Use must and must not (mustn't).

Match the picture of the following measuring tool with the corresponding name. What other tools are needed in incoming inspection?

Vernier calipers

Scales

Measuring tape

Magnifying glass

Micrometers

Microscope

NOTES:

VOCABULARY:

Unit 4 | Lesson 2
Logistics

Listen to this lesson's audio in the course's webpage.

Read the correspondence between Mr. Scott and the Logistics Manager.

To: Logistics Department Manager

From: Joseph Scott

Subject: Incoming Inspection Questions

Hello Italo,
I have a few pending questions from our meeting earlier. I have attached the document. Can you please go over them, and send your answers and observations before the day ends?
Thanks,
Joseph Scott.

To: Joseph Scott

From: Italo Dicaprio, Logistics Department Manager

Subject: Incoming Inspection Inquiries

Greetings Mr. Scott,
As I understand, yesterday's tour was prolonged during your visit to incoming inspection. We were not able to talk in person; however, I hope that I have answered your questions completely. If you have any doubts, let me know.
Your main concerns revolved around our production schedule. As you know, it tells us the time and day we need the components at our warehouse. We have limited space in our production areas. Some components need more inventory. For example, we always need to have critical parts, so that we don't stop the production line because of a part shortage.
Finally, you asked about the customs documents to get clearance for the components. There are two main documents which are an import permit and a pediment.
Your last question is in regards to finances. I have forwarded your question to the Finance Manager.
Kind Regards,
Italo Dicaprio
Logistics Department Manager

As a group, discuss what documents you use at the customs area. Work in pairs. You are going to talk to a customs agent. You need to let them know the information needed to process an import permit and five pediments.

Write a small production schedule for the current month.

Prepositions of Time:

In – Months, Years, Centuries and Long Periods
On – Days and Dates
At – Precise Times

Examples:

In – In 1991, In December, In the Middle Ages, In the 21st Century.
On – On September 16th, On Monday, On Christmas Day.
At – At night, at 9:30, at lunch

NOTES:

VOCABULARY:

Unit 4 | Lesson 3
Finance Department

Listen to this lesson's audio in the course's webpage.

Match the functions of the finance department with the descriptions.

Payroll	Making sure every supplier gets paid on time for every product and service rendered. Scheduling payments.
Taxes	Issuing invoices and tracking them. Making sure that costumers pay them on time.
Accounts Receivable	Making sure all employees are paid on time and according to the hours they worked, including overtime, holidays and bonus.
Reports and Statements	Gathering data to create financial reports for budgets and forecasts. These reports are shown to investors, banks, and other critical people involved in decision making.
Accounts Payable	Following the GAAP standards of accounting principles and procedures to avoid frauds and errors and encourage compliance.
Financial Control	Complying with tax regulations, and other federal, state and local fiscal requirements.

As a group, discuss the following questions.

How do you know the supplier has already shipped the parts?

What does a Purchase Order usually include?

What are the different ways to pay a supplier?

What happens if a supplier does not pay on time?

Who do you talk to if your payment isn't accurate?

What kind of bonus does your company offer?

What other functions are carried out by the finance department?

Important Acronyms:

GAAP: Generally Accepted
Accounting Principles
PO: Purchase Order

Complete the sentences according to the situation.

If the supplier sends the invoice and the PO number, we will _____

If QA _____ the product, we will start packaging and shipping.

If we ask our suppliers for cost savings, our profits will_____

If _____, we will have late payment charges.

If the GAAP principals are not followed, _____

NOTES:

VOCABULARY:

Unit 4 | Lesson 4
Production Department

Listen to this lesson's audio in the course's webpage.

Answer the following questions:

Why does the Planning Department and the Production Department need to work together?

What about the Purchasing Department? The Design Department? Quality Assurance Department?

Have you heard of Lean Manufacturing? What is it and what's your opinion about it?

Some plants have this department divided into Assembly, Finishing, Subassembly, Taping, Wire routing. How is it divided at your plant? What do you do in each area?

Complete these sentences with what applies to your plant. Discuss and compare answers.

1. The suppliers usually want _____, which is the product with the highest volume at our plant.
2. _____ is the person who manages the Production Department.
3. The plant has also a _____ department, where we _____.
4. The production schedule is a plan _____ indicates the exact times for each procedure.
5. We call the Purchasing department _____ we have questions about the materials and the parts of the product.
6. Finished products are sent to _____ where they are inspected before packaging and shipping.
7. The _____ department lets us know when there is a change in a procedure or product.

Read the following lines where Sandy and John describe the products manufactured at their company and write the number in the corresponding bubble.

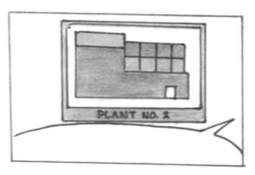

1 This is the area *where* we produce the wheels for the basic line.

2 We also produce the wheels *which* are used for the luxury line.

3 They are made out of a kind of aluminum *that* is high quality for automobiles.

4 We started manufacturing accessories last year *when* we opened the new plant.

5 Greg and Tammy are the engineers *who* supervise this production area.

List of products
manufactured at your plant:

-
-
-
-
-
-
-
-

NOTES:

VOCABULARY:

Appendix

List of Regular and Irregular Verbs
Past and Past Participle

Add	Added	Added
Approve	Approved	Approved
Calculate	Calculated	Calculated
Clean	Cleaned	Cleaned
Close	Closed	Closed
Complete	Completed	Completed
Connect	Connected	Connected
Count	Counted	Counted
Dispose	Disposed	Disposed
Divide	Divided	Divided
Fill Out	Filled out	Filled out
Finish	Finished	Finished
Fit	Fitted	Fitted
Ground	Grounded	Grounded
Include	Included	Included
Inspect	Inspected	Inspected
Introduce	Introduced	Introduced
Join	Joined	Joined
Look	Looked	Looked
Mold	Molded	Molded
Multiply	Multiplied	Multiplied
Notice	Noticed	Noticed
Operate	Operated	Operated
Pack	Packed	Packed
Place	Placed	Placed
Produce	Produced	Produced
Receive	Received	Received
Register	Registered	Registered
Reject	Rejected	Rejected
Route	Routed	Routed
Save	Saved	Saved
Ship	Shipped	Shipped
Snip	Snipped	Snipped
Solder	Soldered	Soldered
Start	Started	Started
Suspend	Suspended	Suspended
Test	Tested	Tested
Trim	Trimmed	Trimmed
Unload	Unloaded	Unloaded
Use	Used	Used

REGULAR:

INFINITIVE	SIMPLE PAST	PAST PARTICIPLE

IRREGULAR:

INFINITIVE	SIMPLE PAST	PAST PARTICIPLE
Is / Are	Was / Were	Been
Become	Became	Become
Begin	Began	Begun
Bend	Bent	Bent
Blow	Blew	Blown
Break	Bought	Bought
Bring	Broke	Broken
Build	Brought	Brought
Buy	Built	Built
Catch	Caught	Caught
Choose	Chose	Chosen
Cut	Cut	Cut
Do	Did	Done
Fall	Fell	Fallen
Feel	Felt	Felt
Find	Fitted	Fitted
Fit	Found	Found
Have	Had	Had
Hold	Held	Held
Make	Made	Made
Put	Put	Put
See	Saw	Seen
Send	Sent	Sent
Take	Took	Taken
Write	Wrote	Written

Do you want to have the **Speak Technical Now** program at your company?

Send a message to programs@speaktechnicalnow.com

Do you want to be a certified English language instructor at **Speak Technical Now**?

Send a message to instructoropportunities@speaktechnicalnow.com

Made in the USA
Columbia, SC
29 September 2022

68200356R00033